THE RIPPLE REVOLUTION

THE RIPPLE REVOLUTION

Changing The World By Changing Yourself. One Breath At A Time.

Steve Neale

Helping Leaders Create Ripples
To Drive Performance Beyond Belief

First edition, 2026
Printed by Amazon KDP
lpszone.com

Book design & layout by Velin@Perseus-Design.com

ISBN Number: 978-1-0676494-0-1

Contents

Dedication

To the two pure souls who mean the world to me - my beautiful wife Nele and our ray of shining light, Xander.

To my father – an angel who passed and whose spirit of kindness is stronger than ever.

To every leader who dares to look within.
To those willing to change the world not through force, but through presence and kindness.
To everyone who believes that small ripples create great waves — this is for you.

Foreword — The Ripple Begins Here

Every movement begins with a moment — a quiet realisation that things cannot continue as they are. For me, that moment came not in a boardroom or a classroom, but in a breath. After years of studying psychology, leading teams, and coaching executives, I began to see a truth I could no longer ignore: no system truly changes until the people within it do. Leadership is not about titles or performance metrics. It's about energy, presence, and how we choose to show up energetically — for ourselves, for others, and for the world. That realisation became the Legacy Leadership Academy — a space for leaders willing to look within, to lead not through force but through awareness and presence. It also became the seed of this book. The Ripple Revolution is more than ideas on a page; it's a call to return to yourself — to remember that change doesn't begin 'out there.' It begins here, now, in what you believe, think, feel, and do. If you let it, this book will not only change how you lead — it will change how you live. Because when one person awakens to the truth of who they are, it sends ripples of awareness through families, teams, organizations, and communities. Together, those ripples become a revolution.

— Steve Neale, November 2025

A Message to the Reader

If you're holding this book in your hands, something within you is already stirring. A desire for the truth.

A question. A quiet knowing. A sense that there must be more than the constant chase — more depth, more connection, more peace. A different world from the one we've been taught to believe is "normal."

This book isn't about theory. It's a guide, a reflection, and a reminder of what you already know deep inside: that real change doesn't begin in the world around you. It begins within you. This isn't about adding more. More knowledge. More skills. More concepts. It's about letting go and shedding those things that interfere with your true essence. It's about unveiling the truth of who you already are and shining that truth brightly into the world round you.

As you move through these pages, take your time.

Pause. Breathe. Reflect.

You'll find ideas to challenge you, exercises to awaken you, and insights to help you lead — not just others, but yourself — with greater compassion, presence and authenticity.

And as you do, remember this simple truth:
Every breath you take is a ripple.
Every choice, every thought, every act of kindness — it all moves outward, shaping the world in ways you may never see.
Thank you for being here. Thank you for choosing awareness.

And thank you for being part of this ripple.

— Steve Neale

Introduction: The Journey Inward – From Striving to Awakening

"As a man changes his own nature, so does the attitude of the world change towards him. We need not wait to see what others do."
Mahatma Gandhi

For most of my life, I chased the dream we're all sold — that glittering version of success.
Titles. Qualifications. Recognition. Wealth. Validation.

On the surface, it looked like I had it all.
But beneath it? Something was missing.

There was a quiet discontent I couldn't name — a sense that despite ticking all the right boxes, I'd somehow lost touch with myself. Like many others,

I had spent years climbing the ladder only to realise it was leaning against the wrong wall.

The truth is, I wasn't failing — I was waking up. And the same may be true for you. Sometimes your apparent failure or sense of unease is an invitation to grow into yourself.

The mental and emotional breakdown I experienced wasn't punishment. It was an invitation. An opportunity.
Life was asking me to slow down, to question, to notice and to reveal the truth.

It didn't happen in one dramatic moment. There was no lightning bolt of clarity. It came gradually, like dawn breaking — uncomfortable, seemingly painful, subtle, frustrating, sometimes lonely and deeply human.

I began to see beyond the mask of ambition and identity. I started to feel again. To reconnect. To ask deeper questions about what truly matters.

That's when the real journey began.

I discovered that our greatest potential lies not in how much we achieve, but in how present, conscious, and connected we become. Emotional intelligence is vital — yes — but it's only part of the picture. What truly transforms leadership is spiritual intelligence: the ability to lead from essence, not ego.

And that's when I learned one of life's hardest truths:

The ego is a beast.

It's clever. Seductive. Restless. It promises safety through control and significance — but left unchecked, it disconnects us from ourselves, from others, and from life itself.

The ego feeds of drama and wants to win and do. The soul wants to love and be.

You don't need to kill your ego. You just need to understand it — to see when it's running the show and to choose instead to lead from something deeper. From love. From gratitude. From kindness.

That's what this book is about.

It's about becoming the kind of leader the world needs now — awake, emotionally and spiritually intelligent, and grounded in awareness. It's about understanding that our most powerful contribution to the world is not what we do, but who we are being.

Change isn't something we impose on others. It's something we embody.

And when we change ourselves, the world around us begins to shift.

That's the Ripple Revolution.

The ripple effect is real. Everything we think, feel, and do sends electromagnetic waves outward — influencing the energy, mood, and potential of everyone and everything we encounter. Whether consciously or not, we're always creating ripples. And the sub-total of those ripples? Collective consciousness.

When we shift our inner world — our beliefs, energy, and intention — we begin to create ripples of calm, trust, and possibility. This is the quiet power of awakened leadership.

The revolution isn't loud. It begins in stillness. It begins with you.

CHAPTER 1

The Taming of the Ego

Most people don't realise they're living in a prison. Not one with iron bars or locked doors, but one made of stories — the stories they've absorbed, inherited, and repeated until they became the apparent truth in the form of beliefs.

We build this prison slowly, often without noticing. From a young age we're taught what success should look like, what behaviour earns approval, and what emotions we're allowed to show. Bit by bit, we form an identity around these expectations, and over time, we forget that the identity is not who we are.

That structure is the ego.

The ego isn't evil. It's simply misunderstood. It was designed to protect you, to help you survive in a world that often feels uncertain or unsafe. It gives you a name, a personality, a false sense of control. But when left unchecked, it can quietly take over — making decisions, driving habits, and colouring your perceptions until you no longer see life as it is, only as your ego interprets it.

The ego loves control and drama. It wants to win, to be right, to be seen. It thrives on comparison and recognition. And while that might help you succeed in the short term, it's also what keeps you disconnected — from yourself, from others, and from what truly matters.

When the ego dominates, we start chasing validation instead of meaning. We become performers, not participants. We act busy, sometimes becoming addicted to the rush of life, even when it costs us our peace or health.

It's easy to mistake this for ambition or drive, but at its core, it's fear. The fear of not being enough. The fear of rejection. The fear of failure.

And fear always narrows our awareness.

It shuts down curiosity, blocks empathy, and replaces presence with protection. It convinces us that life is something to be controlled, not experienced.

So if you want to lead with authenticity, live with purpose, and create genuine impact, you must first learn to see the ego for what it is — a clever storyteller that's forgotten it's not the real author of your life.

You can't destroy the ego, and you don't need to. You just need to understand it. Be aware of it. And tame it.

The TFA Triangle

To learn how to tame your ego, let's look at the mechanics of how your inner world operates — what I call the TFA Triangle:

Thoughts, Feelings, and Actions.

Every experience you have is an interconnected energetic web of thoughts, feelings and actions. Thoughts create electrical activity in your brain, which then releases a chemical response throughout your body — and that chemical response is what you recognise as a feeling. Those feelings, in turn, drive your behaviour.

Thought → Feeling → Action.

That's your TFA Triangle.

And this system is a never ending cycle of energy transfer and can flow in different directions. For example, feelings can trigger thoughts and then actions. Or actions can trigger feelings and then thoughts.

If your thoughts are full of self-criticism or fear, your feelings will reflect that — anxious, tense, defensive. And those feelings drive behaviours that reinforce the very reality you want to escape.

But change one corner of the triangle, and everything shifts.

When you change your thoughts, you shift your feelings. When you change your feelings, you shift your actions. And when you change your actions, you change your life.

And you can break the loop at any point in the triangle — because they all feed each other.

To start to process of habitual looping, there is a fundamental truth that many people fail to realise:

You are not your thoughts, feelings, or actions.
You are the awareness behind them — the one with the power to choose.

That awareness is your higher consciousness — the part of you that can pause, reflect, and choose. The ego reacts. Awareness responds. And that one distinction changes everything.

Mindfulness: The Art of Awareness

This is where mindfulness comes in — not as a buzzword or a relaxation technique, but as a lifelong skill of self-observation.

Mindfulness allows you to take a step back from the constant chatter in your head and notice what's really going on. It's not about trying to silence the mind or control emotions; it's about watching them with curiosity instead of criticism.

Imagine sitting beside a river and watching leaves drift past on the surface. Each leaf is a thought, a feeling, a reaction. You don't need to chase them or label them or understand them. You just watch them float by.

That's mindfulness in action.

Next time you catch yourself thinking, "I'm not good enough," or "They don't appreciate me," pause. Take a slow breath. Acknowledge the thought without judging it. "There's a thought about not being enough," you might say to yourself. The moment you do that, you've shifted from being in the thought to being the observer of it — and that's the place where your power lies.

Do the same with emotions. When frustration, sadness, or anger arises, try describing it rather than becoming it. Give it form — a colour, a texture, a shape. "This feels heavy, tight, red." The moment you describe it, you create space between you and the emotion. And in that space, you find choice.

Even your actions can be seen this way. When you catch yourself reacting in a way that doesn't serve you — snapping at someone, withdrawing, overworking — step back afterwards and reflect gently. "What was really going on there? What need wasn't being met? What could I do differently next time?"

This is not self-criticism. It's self-awareness in practice. And awareness is always the first step to change.

You Are the Observer

Here's what makes this so transformative.

Every thought you think sends a wave of electrical energy through your brain and into the energetic field around you. Every emotion you feel releases chemicals that affect your body and environment. Every action you take sends kinetic energy within and into the world around you.

You are an energetic being — constantly creating ripples of change in yourself and in the world around you, whether you realise it or not.

When you learn to observe your own thoughts, feelings, and actions, you can begin to direct those ripples consciously. You become intentional and responsive instead of impulsive and reactive. You become the calm centre in the middle of chaos — the one who can lead with clarity when others are lost in noise.

This is what it means to tame the ego. You don't destroy it; you take back the driver's seat.

No longer a victim of emotion or circumstance, you become the creator of your own experience. And in that shift from victim to creator, you begin to choose peace instead of proving, understanding instead of control, compassion instead of competition.

And from that state of awareness, everything changes.

REFLECTION EXERCISE

Take a few minutes right now to reflect on the following:

What thoughts have you been replaying lately?

How do those thoughts make you feel in your body?

What behaviours or habits have followed those feelings?

If you were to change just one thought today, what might shift as a result?

Write down your answers without editing them. Be honest. Then take a slow, deep breath, and remind yourself:

"I am the observer of my thoughts, feelings, and actions — therefore, I am."

Because the moment you step back from the noise and see yourself clearly, you stop being controlled by the ego. You become conscious. You become free to choose.

And that's where the ripple begins.

CHAPTER 2

Finding Your True Potential

For most of your life, you've been told a story about who you are — and what you're capable of.
It sounded convincing. It came from teachers, parents, culture, and even science.

It said that you are largely fixed. That your potential is determined by your genes, your upbringing, or your personality. That you are who you are — and the best you can do is make the most of it.

It's a neat story. Predictable. Safe.
And it's completely wrong.

You are not a static being trapped by your past. You are a living, breathing, evolving system of energy, emotion, and consciousness — constantly reshaping yourself with every thought you think, every feeling you generate, and every action you take.

The science now backs this up. For decades, biology told us our DNA was destiny — a rigid code written before we were born. But as cell biologist Dr. Bruce Lipton revealed in The Biology of Belief, genes don't control your life; your beliefs do.

He showed that your DNA is not a fixed script, but a dynamic system that responds to signals from your environment. And here's the key: you are that environment.

Every cell in your body listens to what you believe, what you feel, and how you think. When you are stressed, fearful, or self-critical, your body releases chemical messengers that tell your cells to protect and defend. But when you are calm, grateful, and open, your body sends signals of safety — inviting growth, healing, and expansion.

So you are not a victim of biology.
You are the author of it.

The Inner Garden

Think of yourself as a garden.
Your thoughts are the sunlight. Your emotions are the water. Your actions are the soil.

If your inner environment is full of negativity, pressure, and fear, the garden withers. Nothing thrives in toxicity. But when you cultivate awareness, self-compassion, and belief in possibility, growth becomes inevitable.

Everything you allow into your world shapes your potential — not just what you eat or how you move, but what you read, who you spend time with, where you spend your time, the conversations you engage in, and the energy you bring into every moment.

Every thought, every image, every word is a signal to your system.
Your nervous system listens. Your cells respond.

That's why so many people feel stuck. It's not because they're broken. It's because they've been feeding their mind and body with the wrong signals for too long.

When you start shifting those signals — when you begin to think more consciously, feel more intentionally, and act more purposefully — you literally begin to change your biology.

You move from survival into growth.

From Programmed to Conscious

Most people live on autopilot. Research suggests that around 95-99% of our daily behaviour is unconscious — a repetition of yesterday's habits, thoughts, and emotional responses. We think we're choosing freely, but in truth, we're mostly repeating patterns we didn't consciously design.

It's not that people don't want to change — they just don't know how to interrupt the pattern.

But awareness is the disruptor.

When you start to see your patterns — when you notice the beliefs, stories, and emotions driving them — you reclaim choice. That's when growth begins.

It's like waking from a dream. At first it's disorienting. You notice how much of your life was driven by unconscious scripts — by "shoulds," by approval-seeking, by avoidance of discomfort. But slowly, you start to see new possibilities.

You realise that change doesn't start with effort. It starts with awareness.
And awareness always begins with a pause.

That pause is the space between stimulus and reaction or response — the space where your power lives.

The Signals You Send

Your mind is like a broadcast tower, constantly transmitting signals into the world — through your thoughts, your tone, your body language, and your energy.

If you're sending out frustration, people will feel it.
If you're sending out calm confidence, they'll feel that too.

And because we live in a connected field of energy, the signals you emit don't just affect others — they also loop back into your own system, reinforcing the reality you experience.

That's the science behind what's often called the law of resonance or law of attraction.
It's not mystical; it's physics.

You don't attract what you want — you attract what you are.
Your outer world mirrors your inner world.

So when you change the signal you send — through your thoughts, your emotions, your actions — you start to change the field around you.

Activating Your Potential

Your potential isn't something you have to find. It's something you activate.

And the way to do that isn't through one huge leap or radical change — it's through small, consistent actions that align your energy every day.

Start by asking simple, mindful questions:

What thoughts am I choosing to focus on today?

What emotions am I carrying into my meetings, my family, my work?

What actions will nourish my growth instead of feeding my fear?

Then take one small step — just one — in the direction of who you want to become.

This is the principle of Kaizen — the Japanese philosophy of continuous, incremental improvement. A single conscious breath, a moment of gratitude, a short walk in nature, a conversation held with more presence — these micro-shifts compound over time into profound transformation.

You don't need to overhaul your life in one grand act of willpower. You simply need to keep turning towards awareness, one small step at a time.

That's how potential becomes performance.
That's how intention becomes impact.
That's how change becomes who you are.

REFLECTION EXERCISE

Pause for a few minutes and reflect:

Where in your life do you still feel limited or stuck or frustrated? In relationships, work, health, environment, finances?

What beliefs or stories might be creating this situation for you and keeping you stuck there?

What's one small signal you could change today — one new thought, feeling, or action — that would move you from survival into growth?

Write it down.
Then act on it, no matter how small it seems.

Because potential isn't waiting to be discovered.

It's waiting to be lived.

And the moment you begin to change the signals you send — to yourself, to others, to the world — you begin to shape a different reality.

That's when you stop existing as a reaction to life, and start living as a conscious creator of it.

And that's where your ripple begins to expand.

CHAPTER 3

Changing the World from the Inside Out

We live in a culture obsessed with doing.
Every day, people rush to fix, to solve, to improve.
We tick off lists, chase deadlines, and measure our worth by productivity.

It sounds noble — but most of the time, it's just noise.

Because when we're constantly doing, we rarely stop to ask why.
And without "why," even the busiest life can feel hollow.

The truth is, you can't change the world effectively if you're disconnected from yourself.
You can't lead with authenticity if you don't understand what drives you.

You can't inspire others if you're running on autopilot, fuelled by stress and ego instead of purpose and awareness.

Real change — the kind that lasts — always begins from within.

It begins when you stop trying to control the external world, and start mastering the internal one.
It begins when you shift from reaction to reflection, from striving to stillness, from proving to presence.

You don't need to fix the world.
You need to align with yourself.

Start with Why

Leadership thinker Simon Sinek popularised the idea of starting with why — and it remains one of the simplest yet most powerful models of human motivation.

At the core of Sinek's Golden Circle are three layers:

Why – your core purpose or belief.

How – your values and uniqueness

What – your actions and outcomes.

Most people, and most organisations, live from the outside in.
They start with what they do — the projects, the targets, the products — and only later, if ever, do they ask why.

But the most inspiring leaders and movements operate from the inside out.
They start with why, allowing purpose to shape every decision, every conversation, every strategy.

This principle applies far beyond leadership or business. It's a way of living. And it's way bigger than any individual, ego or selfish pursuit of gain.

When you live from your why, your life gains coherence. Your actions start to feel meaningful, not mechanical. You stop chasing and start creating.

Your why is your compass and it keeps you aligned when everything around you shifts.

But purpose can't just live in your head.
It must be embodied.

Be → Do → Have

This is an idea I first heard from the author and product creator Peter Thomson.

Most people live by the formula: Have → Do → Be.

"If I have more money, I can do more of what I love, and then I'll be happy."

"If I have more recognition, I can do meaningful work, and then I'll be fulfilled."

It sounds logical. But it's backwards.

The inside-out approach reverses this formula:
Be → Do → Have.

Be first.
Then do.
Then have.

When you start by being — by aligning your internal state with awareness, values, presence, gratitude and authenticity — the doing becomes clearer, more natural, and the results follow.

Being is the foundation.
Doing is the expression.
Having is the outcome.

You can't build sustainable success or meaningful change from a state of chaos, fear, or ego. You might achieve short-term results, but you'll most likely burn out in the process.

Start by being present, purposeful and grounded. Then let your actions flow from that space.

The ego wants you to prove your worth by doing. Your consciousness reminds you that your worth already exists — and your doing is simply an expression of that truth.

When the Ego Wears a Halo

Here's the tricky part.
Even when we think we're being "spiritual," the ego can sneak back in through the side door.

It whispers things like:

"I'll be the most generous."
"I'll be the most conscious."
"I'll be the one who helps everyone else."

"I'm so spiritual."

It sounds virtuous. But it's still ego — just dressed in spiritual clothes.

Real transformation isn't about appearing enlightened or thinking you are in some way special. It's about staying humble, present, and curious.
It's about living your truth without needing to prove it.

That's what I call embodied awareness — where what you believe internally and how you behave externally are one and the same.

When you reach that level of congruence, your presence becomes magnetic. People feel it before they understand it.

It's not about what you say. It's about the energy you bring.

The Power of Presence

Presence may appear to be the opposite of high level performance. But ironically, it often leads to better results.
It's the moment when you stop trying to be impressive and start being real.

When you're fully present, you stop living in the mental noise of past regrets or future anxieties. You meet people where they are — here, now.

And something extraordinary happens.
Your energy shifts.
People relax around you.
They open up.
They trust.

That's the ripple in action.

Presence is contagious. It regulates your nervous systems, lowers tension, and creates psychological safety. That's why great leaders are remembered not for what they achieved, but for how people felt around them.

When you lead from presence, you stop transmitting fear and start radiating calm. And calm is not passive – it's powerful.

It's the still point around which transformation happens.

The Real Revolution

The world doesn't need more busyness or more noise.
It needs more consciousness. More awareness.

It needs people who are awake enough to notice what's happening inside them before they react to what's happening around them.

It needs leaders who don't just change policies, but change energy — who understand that the outer world is a reflection of our collective inner state.

That's the real revolution.

It's not a battle to be fought. It's a shift to be lived.

It begins every time you choose awareness over autopilot.
Compassion over control.
Stillness over striving.

That's how you can change the world — one breath at a time.

REFLECTION EXERCISE

Pause and reflect for a few minutes:

Where in your life are you living from "doing" instead of "being"?

What would shift if you led with presence rather than pressure?

What's one situation this week where you could practise awareness before reaction?

Write your answers down.
Keep them simple.
Then read them slowly.

Because the moment you return to awareness, you reconnect with your why.
And when you lead from why, the world around you begins to change naturally.

CHAPTER 4

The Quantum Field and the Ripple Effect (From "woo-woo" to science)

When you drop a pebble into a still pond, you don't need to push the ripples.
They expand naturally — outward, effortlessly, perfectly balanced.

That's how you really work. You are the pebble in the pond of life.

In leadership, in life, in every interaction you have, you're dropping energetic pebbles — thoughts, emotions, actions— into the quantum field that connects us all. And those ripples spread, whether you're aware of them or not.

Science is finally catching up with what ancient wisdom has always known: everything is connected. The same energy that moves through stars and oceans moves through you. The same field that holds galaxies together also holds your thoughts, your emotions, and your choices.

You are not separate from life — you are life expressing itself in human form.

Energy, Frequency, and Emotion

At the deepest level, everything you experience is energy vibrating at different frequencies. Your body, your words, even your thoughts — all of it is energy in motion.

When physicists look into the smallest particles of matter, they don't find solid objects. They find that each cell in your body is 99.99% nothing. Space. And what fills that space? Waves of energy. Energy that becomes matter only when observed.

This means that reality isn't fixed. It's fluid, responsive, and deeply influenced by consciousness.

In other words, you are a participant in creation, not just an observer.

Your emotions are frequencies.
Gratitude, love, compassion — high frequencies that expand your energy field.
Fear, anger, guilt — low frequencies that contract it.

Every time you choose a thought, you're tuning your internal frequency, and that frequency determines the kind of experiences, people, and opportunities you attract.

This isn't mysticism. It's resonance.

Just like a tuning fork vibrates in harmony with another at the same pitch, your emotional state resonates with the experiences that match its vibration.

So if you're operating from fear, you'll find more reasons to be afraid.
If you're living in gratitude, you'll see more to be thankful for.

What you focus on expands — not because the world changes instantly, but because your perception, your biology, and your behaviour align with what you expect to see.

The Science of Possibility

Quantum physics has shown that particles exist in multiple states at once — until they are observed. This is called the "observer effect." It suggests that consciousness itself plays a role in shaping reality.

In simple terms, your attention collapses potential into form.
Where your focus goes, energy flows.

So when you repeatedly focus on fear, failure, or limitation, you give those possibilities more energy. But when you focus on opportunity, purpose, and possibility, you collapse a different version of reality into being.

That's not wishful thinking. It's quantum engagement.

Every decision, every thought, every act of awareness is an instruction to the field around you. And because the field is connected, your energy doesn't stop with you. It ripples outward — affecting others, subtly but powerfully.

That's why great leaders don't just manage people — they manage energy.

They understand that their emotional state sets the tone for their team, their family, their organisation.

They take responsibility not just for what they do, but for how they show up.

The Ripple Principle

The Ripple Principle is simple but profound:
Every internal shift creates an external impact.

Your inner state is the cause. Your outer experience is the effect.

Most people try to change the world by rearranging the outer world — working harder, managing others, forcing results. But that's like trying to calm the surface of a lake by pushing down the waves. It doesn't work.

Real change begins within.
When you shift your thoughts, your energy, and your emotional vibration, the world responds.

You've felt this before.

You walk into a room after an argument, and you can feel the tension — even if no one says a word. Or you meet someone grounded and open, and somehow, your shoulders drop, your breathing slows, and you feel safe.

That's the ripple effect in action.

Your energy speaks before you do.
Your presence either creates harmony or discord in the field.

So the most powerful thing you can do for the world is to become responsible for the energy you bring to it.

From Reaction to Resonance

Most of us spend our lives reacting to external events — to people, to problems, to pressures.
But the moment you realise you're influencing the field as much as it's influencing you, the dynamic changes completely.

You stop reacting.
You start resonating.

Instead of trying to control outcomes, you focus on alignment — bringing your energy into coherence so that your thoughts, feelings, and actions are congruent.

When your inner world is aligned, your outer world begins to mirror that harmony.

That's why mindfulness, meditation, and conscious breathing aren't luxuries for busy leaders — they're necessities. They bring your energy field into coherence, allowing you to influence with calm, clarity, and compassion instead of chaos.

Your presence becomes your greatest tool.

Creating Coherence

Researchers at the HeartMath Institute have shown that the heart generates the largest electromagnetic field in the body — one that can be measured several feet away. When your emotions are in harmony — when you feel appreciation, love, or gratitude — your heart rhythm becomes coherent, sending stable, synchronised signals throughout your body and beyond.

That coherence affects others.

When you're calm and centred, you literally help regulate the nervous systems of people around you. Their hearts and brains start to synchronise with yours. This isn't metaphor — it's measurable.

So if you want to lead with influence, start by leading your energy.

Breathe deeply. Feel your heart. Choose the frequency you wish to transmit.

Because every breath, every thought, every heartbeat is a message to the field.

And the more conscious that message becomes, the stronger your ripple grows.

REFLECTION EXERCISE

Take a few minutes to practise coherence right now.

Sit quietly. Bring your attention to your breath.

Focus on your heart area — imagine you're breathing through it.

As you breathe, recall something or someone you deeply appreciate. Feel that emotion expand.

Stay with that feeling for a few minutes, noticing how your body shifts.

Now reflect on these questions:

What kind of energy have I been transmitting lately?

What ripple have I been creating around me — at home, at work, in the world?

What would change if I became more intentional with the energy I bring into every space?

Write your reflections. Be honest, but gentle.

Then breathe once more — slowly, fully — and remind yourself:

"Every thought, every feeling, every action is a ripple.
The question is — what kind of ripple am I creating?"

CHAPTER 5

Love or Fear: The Two Energies That Shape Everything

At the root of every thought, feeling, and behaviour lie only two fundamental energies: love and fear.

Every emotion you've ever experienced — joy, gratitude, compassion, curiosity — stems from love. Every emotion that constricts — anger, anxiety, shame, guilt, frustration — stems from fear.

Every decision you make, every conversation you have, every way you show up in the world comes down to which of these two energies is running the show.

Most people live their entire lives reacting from fear, yet call it something else.

They say they're being "practical," "realistic," or "careful." But underneath those words, fear is quietly steering the wheel — fear of failure, fear of rejection, fear of not being enough.

Love and fear are not opposites on a moral scale; they are simply different frequencies of energy. Fear contracts. Love expands. Fear protects. Love connects. Fear isolates. Love unites.

The real art of emotional intelligence is learning to recognise which one is driving you — and then choosing consciously.

How Fear Disguises Itself

Fear is clever. It rarely walks into the room and introduces itself.
It wears masks — ambition, control, judgment, even perfectionism.

It whispers that if you can just achieve one more thing, get one more approval, or avoid one more mistake, you'll finally be safe.

But fear's promises are empty. It gives you the illusion of safety while quietly draining your vitality, creativity, and joy.

You can recognise fear by its symptoms: tension in your body, defensiveness in your tone, urgency in your decisions. It makes you want to close down, to prove, to hide, or to control.

It's not your enemy — it's just a signal.
It's your system's way of saying, "Something here feels uncertain."

And uncertainty, if approached with awareness, is not a threat. It's an invitation.

The Wisdom of Love

Love doesn't mean softness or surrender.
It means openness, connection, and courage.

Love is what allows you to face reality without flinching — to acknowledge pain, to sit with discomfort, and to respond with compassion instead of defence.

Where fear says, "Protect yourself," love says, "Expand yourself."

In leadership, love shows up as empathy, trust, and presence. It's the courage to listen deeply, even when it's uncomfortable. It's the choice to assume positive intent. It's the ability to stay calm when others react.

When you lead from love, people feel safe to bring their whole selves to the table. They stop guarding their image and start offering their insight. That's where creativity and collaboration flourish.

Love isn't sentimental. It's strategic. It creates conditions for growth.

In neuroscience terms, love activates the parasympathetic nervous system — the state of safety and connection where learning and innovation thrive. Fear, on the other hand, triggers the sympathetic system — fight, flight, or freeze — where creativity shuts down and defensiveness rises.

So when you choose love over fear, you're not just being kind — you're being effective.

The Moment of Choice

Every moment gives you a chance to choose which energy to follow.

When a challenge appears, you can contract in fear or expand in love.
When someone criticises you, you can defend your ego or stay open to learn.
When uncertainty looms, you can resist or you can trust.

This is not about pretending everything is positive or suppressing difficult emotions. It's about recognising that fear will always be there — and you can still choose love anyway.

Choosing love doesn't mean you never feel fear; it means you don't let fear drive.

It's like driving a car with fear sitting in the passenger seat. You can listen to what it has to say — "Slow down," "Be careful," "Watch the road" — but you don't hand it the keys.

The more you practise this choice, the easier it becomes. Eventually, it becomes your new default — your natural state.

Fear as a Teacher

When fear arises, most people try to push it away. But what if fear isn't something to fight, but something to understand?

Fear is not an obstacle to growth — it's a doorway.

Every fear you face reveals a part of you that's asking for attention, compassion, and healing. When you meet fear with curiosity instead of avoidance, it begins to dissolve.

Next time you feel fear, pause.
Ask:

What is this feeling trying to protect me from?

What belief is it connected to?

What would love do here?

Often, the simple act of acknowledging fear with compassion is enough to transform it. Because what fear fears most… is awareness.

The Leadership Ripple

A leader's energy doesn't just affect them — it sets the tone for everyone around them.

If you lead from fear, your team mirrors it. They become cautious, risk-averse, hesitant to speak. But if you lead from love — from calm confidence and stability — people rise. They become braver, more collaborative, more creative.

This is why emotional energy is the most powerful leadership tool you have.

Your calm becomes contagious. Your presence regulates the nervous systems of others.

When you walk into a room grounded in love, the energy changes before you say a word.

You've probably seen it.
That quiet leader whose very presence settles the chaos.
That colleague who doesn't need to raise their voice to command respect.

That's love in action — power without force.

REFLECTION EXERCISE

Take a few moments of stillness.
Close your eyes. Breathe slowly.

Ask yourself:

Where in my life or work am I being led by fear right now?

What would it look like if I approached that situation from love instead?

How would I speak, think, or act differently if love were the energy behind it?

Write what comes up. Don't overthink it. Just notice.

Then place your hand over your heart and say quietly:

"In this moment, I choose love."

Because every time you make that choice — one thought, one breath, one interaction at a time — you shift your energy, and the world shifts with you.

That's not philosophy. That's physics.
And that's what makes The Ripple Revolution real.

CHAPTER 6

Gratitude, Growth and the Art of Letting Go

Every moment you hold onto what no longer serves you — an old belief, a past hurt, a fixed identity — you stop yourself from growing.
And yet, we all do it.

We cling to the familiar because it feels safe. Even when that "safety" quietly suffocates us.

But growth and safety rarely live in the same room.

If you want to evolve — as a leader, as a partner, as a human being — you must learn the art of letting go. Letting go is not about losing control. It's about releasing resistance.

It's about trusting that the space left behind by what you release will be filled with something better, something more aligned, something true.

That trust begins with gratitude.

The Alchemy of Gratitude

Gratitude is the emotional bridge between fear and love.
It transforms scarcity into abundance, frustration into peace, and chaos into clarity.

When you practise gratitude, you train your mind to look for what's right rather than what's wrong. You shift your energy from lack to fullness.

Neuroscience shows that consistent gratitude practice strengthens the neural pathways associated with optimism, resilience, and emotional regulation. It even alters the chemistry of your body — increasing dopamine and serotonin, your natural feel-good neurotransmitters.

In other words, gratitude literally rewires your brain for wellbeing.

But this isn't about forcing yourself to be positive. It's about presence — noticing the small, quiet miracles that are already here.

The warmth of sunlight.
The rhythm of your breath.
The laughter of someone you love.
The privilege of being alive, right now, in this moment.

Gratitude doesn't require perfection.
It requires awareness.

And the more aware you become, the more there is to be grateful for.

The Science of Growth

Growth is not a straight line.
It's a spiral.

You revisit lessons, old patterns, familiar triggers — each time from a slightly higher perspective.

As Abraham Maslow suggested, growth is a choice we make moment by moment:
"You will either step forward into growth or step back into safety."

But growth is rarely comfortable.
It challenges your ego, your routines, your sense of control.

That's why most people resist it — not because they don't want to grow, but because they don't want to feel the uncertainty that growth demands.

Yet uncertainty is the soil of transformation.

Your nervous system may interpret uncertainty as danger, but your soul knows it as potential. The key is learning to stay calm and open in the midst of the unknown.

That's where gratitude becomes your anchor — the emotional signal that says, "Even though I can't see the full picture, I trust the process."

The Power of Letting Go

Letting go is not weakness. It's wisdom.
It's knowing the difference between what's yours to carry and what isn't.

We often mistake attachment for love, control for strength, and endurance for resilience. But true resilience isn't about holding on tighter — it's about knowing when to release.

You can't receive new experiences if your hands are clenched around old ones.
You can't become your next self while defending your current one.

When you let go of what no longer aligns, you don't lose yourself — you reveal yourself.

You clear space for something higher to emerge.

How to Practise Letting Go

Acknowledge the Weight
Notice what feels heavy in your life right now.
A relationship? A belief? A habit?
Don't judge it — just recognise it.

Name the Fear Beneath It
Ask yourself, "What am I afraid will happen if I release this?"
Often, the fear is not about the loss — it's about the void.
But remember, the void is fertile ground.

Replace Resistance with Gratitude
Thank whatever you're releasing for what it taught you.
Even pain has been a teacher.
When you release with gratitude, you close the loop of learning.

Breathe It Out
Literally.
On each exhale, imagine letting the weight drift away.
Feel yourself becoming lighter, freer, more open.

This is not a one-time ritual. It's a lifelong practice — a rhythm of expansion.

The Gratitude–Growth Loop

Gratitude grounds you. Growth stretches you. Letting go frees you.

Together, they form a self-renewing cycle — one that keeps you evolving without burning out.

Gratitude without growth becomes complacency.
Growth without gratitude becomes striving.
Letting go without either becomes emptiness.

But when the three work together, something extraordinary happens:
You begin to live in flow.

Life no longer feels like a series of struggles to overcome, but a movement to dance with.
Challenges still come — but they meet a wiser, softer you.

Leadership in Flow

In leadership, gratitude changes the energy of entire teams.
A thank you, sincerely given, activates trust.
Appreciation turns compliance into commitment.

Growth, meanwhile, demands courage — the willingness to be wrong, to learn publicly, to keep evolving.

And letting go? That's the quiet strength of a conscious leader — knowing when to release control, delegate, or allow others to shine.

This kind of leadership doesn't just achieve results.
It awakens potential.
It creates ripples of emotional safety and creative flow that extend far beyond the boardroom.

REFLECTION EXERCISE

Take a quiet moment.
Place your hand on your heart.
Breathe slowly.

Then write down:

Three things you're grateful for today.

One area of your life that's asking for growth.

One thing you're ready to release.

Read them out loud — gently, without rush.
Then say to yourself:

"I am grateful for what was.
I am growing into what's next.
I let go of what no longer serves."

And as you breathe, imagine that energy rippling outward — into your relationships, your work, your world.

Because when gratitude fuels growth, and letting go becomes natural, you stop fighting life.
You start flowing with it.
And that's when your true power begins to unfold.

CHAPTER 7

The Energy of Action: From Intention to Impact

Action is energy made visible.
It's the bridge between thought and reality — between who you are and what you bring into the world.

But not all action is equal.
Some actions drain you. Others energise you.
Some create noise. Others create change.

In a world obsessed with productivity, it's easy to confuse movement with progress.
But busyness isn't brilliance. And speed isn't success.

Real impact — the kind that ripples far beyond you — doesn't come from doing more.
It comes from acting consciously.

The Power of Aligned Action

Alignment is the meeting point between your values, your purpose, and your behaviour.
When these three are in harmony, your actions carry a different kind of power — quiet, focused, unstoppable.

People can feel it.
They might not know why, but they sense integrity in your presence. Your words land deeper. Your work resonates further.

When your actions are aligned with your deeper self, effort transforms into flow.

This is not mystical — it's energetic coherence.
Your thoughts, emotions, and movements vibrate in the same direction.
And when your internal signal is coherent, the universe, or if you prefer, the world around you, responds in kind.

You become what psychologist Mihaly Csikszentmihalyi called a "channel of flow" — fully immersed, present, productive, and alive.

Intention: The Invisible Engine

Every action begins as an intention.
Before you move your body, you move your energy.

An intention is not a wish or a to-do list item. It's a frequency — a felt sense of what you want to create.

If you act without conscious intention, you scatter your energy. You move, but without direction.
But when you infuse your actions with intention, every step becomes meaningful.

It's like the difference between wandering and walking with purpose.

Even small, mundane tasks — sending an email, making a call, cleaning the kitchen — become acts of presence when you approach them intentionally.

Ask yourself before acting:

"What energy am I bringing into this?"

The answer changes everything.

The 1% Rule: Small Acts, Massive Ripples

You don't need to change your entire life overnight. Transformation is not an event — it's a rhythm.

The Japanese philosophy of Kaizen teaches that consistent 1% improvements compound into extraordinary results.

When you make small, conscious adjustments daily — to your habits, your conversations, your mindset — you gradually reshape the course of your life.

As James Clear wrote in Atomic Habits:

"You do not rise to the level of your goals. You fall to the level of your systems."

So the goal is not to set bigger goals.
The goal is to create better systems — rituals and routines that align your energy with your purpose.

Because when you do that, improvement becomes effortless.

Every breath, every choice, every action becomes part of your ripple.

Presence in Motion

One of the greatest misconceptions in leadership and life is that presence and performance are opposites.
That you can either be mindful or productive.
Still or successful.

But true mastery is the fusion of the two — being calm in the midst of movement.

You can send an email mindfully.
You can speak to a team with presence.
You can make a decision with awareness.

In fact, that's where excellence lives.

When you act from stillness, your energy is clean — free from urgency, fear, or ego.
And clean energy creates clear impact.

It's not about slowing down; it's about moving with consciousness.

As martial arts master Bruce Lee said,

"The successful warrior is the average man, with laser-like focus."

Presence sharpens action. It turns movement into mastery.

Humanity Plus Thinking

Before you act, ask yourself three questions:

Is this good for me?

Is this good for others?

Is this good for the planet?

If the answer is yes to all three, you're practising what I call Humanity Plus Thinking — creating value that expands, not contracts.

Every product, decision, conversation, and creation becomes a contribution.
Your ripple becomes regenerative.

This is conscious capitalism. Conscious leadership. Conscious living.
Not driven by ego, but by evolution.

Resistance: The Invisible Barrier

Every meaningful action meets resistance.
You'll feel it as hesitation, procrastination, or fear.

That's not a sign you're off track — it's a sign you're growing.

Resistance is simply the ego's way of saying, "I'm scared of change."

You overcome resistance not by fighting it, but by moving through it gently.

Take one small, aligned step.
Then another.
And another.

Momentum builds trust. Trust builds confidence.
And confidence turns resistance into resilience.

The hardest part of any journey is the first conscious step.

REFLECTION EXERCISE

Take five minutes.
Breathe slowly. Feel your body grounded where you sit.

Then write down:

What is one small action I can take today that aligns with my purpose?

What energy will I bring into that action — fear or love?

Who might benefit from this ripple, beyond me?

When you've written your answers, take a deep breath.

Then act.

Even the smallest step, taken with clear intention and steady presence, can start a ripple that moves through families, teams, communities — even generations.

Because true leadership isn't measured by how much you do.
It's measured by the quality of consciousness you bring to what you do.

When you combine intention, alignment, and love —
your every action becomes a prayer,
your work becomes your meditation,
and your life becomes your legacy.

That's the energy of action.
That's impact.
That's the ripple at work.

CHAPTER 8

The Eight Essentials of Lasting Change

Change is not a single event — it's a living process.
It's not something that happens to you. (I'm a passive victim)
It's something that happens through you. (I'm a connected creator)

And yet, so many people struggle with it. They start with enthusiasm, only to lose momentum. They set goals, only to watch them fade into "maybe next year."

The reason isn't laziness. It's misalignment.
Most people try to change through willpower alone — through force, pressure, or guilt.
But real transformation doesn't come from force. It comes from flow.

When your energy, emotion, and environment are aligned with your deeper purpose, change becomes natural. Effortless. Sustainable.

Over the years, I've distilled this into what I call **The Eight Essentials of Lasting Change** — eight inner and outer shifts that create transformation that endures.

1. Vision and Emotional Alignment

Everything begins with vision.
But not just a logical, intellectual picture — an emotional one.

You must be able to feel the life you want to create. See it vividly. Feel it fully.

Close your eyes and imagine yourself six months or a year from now. What does your ideal life look like? How do you move, speak, and breathe?
Who are you becoming?

If your vision doesn't stir emotion, it won't generate movement.

Emotion is energy in motion.
It's what turns an idea into action.

So connect your vision to something that matters — your values, your purpose, your "why."
Let your heart lead and your mind follow.

> "When you are inspired by a great purpose,
> all your thoughts break their bonds."
> — Patanjali

2. Awareness of Now and Presence

If vision is the destination, awareness is the map.

You can't move forward unless you know where you stand.

Self-awareness means noticing your thoughts, your habits, your emotions — not to judge them, but to understand them.

Presence is the ability to observe without reacting.
It gives you perspective. It gives you choice.

So pause often.
Breathe deeply.
Ask yourself: "What's really happening right now — in me, not just around me?"

The more aware you become of the present moment, the more power you have to shape the next one.

And in that presence you create a realistic understanding of where you are at currently in relation to your chosen goal. And we need this level of brutal honesty in order to move forwards. This involved being honest with yourself and being genuinely open to the constructive feedback of others. It cancels out avoidance and delusion and ensures we start at a realistic place in the chosen change journey.

3. Co-Creation

Change isn't meant to be a solo act.

Every great transformation happens in relationship — with mentors, coaches, peers, or communities who hold space for your evolution.

As Carl Jung said, "The meeting of two personalities is like the contact of two chemical substances: if there is any reaction, both are transformed."

Find someone who challenges you and champions you in equal measure.

Co-create your plan with them. Let them mirror your blind spots and celebrate your breakthroughs.

Because while self-reflection brings awareness, connection brings acceleration.

4. Accountability to Others

This is a natural accompaniment to step 3.

Accountability is not about pressure — it's about partnership.

When you tell someone your goal, it becomes real. When you know someone will ask about your progress, your brain interprets that as commitment.

That's why coaching, peer partnerships, and leadership programmes work.
They keep you walking your talk.

So choose accountability that feels supportive, not punitive.
Find people who remind you of your potential, not your failures.

You're not being watched. You're being witnessed and supported.

5. Responsibility to Self

Accountability is external.
Responsibility is internal.

It's the moment you stop outsourcing your results to circumstance and take full ownership of your energy, your effort, and your choices. It's the point you start to notice your internal excuses and chose not to allow them to decide your actions. Things like, "well just one cake won't hurt," or "I guess it's ok if I don't do it all the time. After all, I'm only human."

It's the quiet strength of saying,

"This is my life. This is my ripple. I own it."

You can't control the world, but you can always control how you respond to it.

That's where freedom begins.

6. Celebrate Bright Spots

Your brain is wired to focus on problems. It's a survival mechanism — useful in a jungle, less so in a boardroom.

If you want to rewire your mind for growth, you must train it to notice what's working.

Celebration isn't ego. It's reinforcement.
When you acknowledge progress, however small, you strengthen the neural pathways associated with success.

So celebrate often.
Name the wins. Share them. Feel them.

Because what you celebrate expands — in your mind, your team, and your energy field.

7. Community and Collective Motivation

You rise faster when you rise together.

Individual motivation can be powerful, but collective motivation is magnetic.
When you're surrounded by people who are growing, their energy amplifies yours.

This is the power of community — the shared space where transformation becomes culture.

That is what the Legacy Leadership Academy is all about: a space for conscious leaders to grow together, to share breakthroughs, to ripple change across industries and lives.

Because when one person raises their energy, everyone around them benefits.
When a whole group does it — a revolution begins.

8. Reflection and Integration

Without reflection, change becomes noise.
Without integration, growth fades.

Reflection is where learning becomes wisdom.

Set aside time each week to look back with curiosity, not criticism.
Ask:

What shifted this week?

What worked?

What challenged me?

What am I grateful for?

Then integrate the insights into your next actions. That's how growth compounds — not through perfection, but through awareness and adjustment.

The Rhythm of Real Change

Change is not about intensity.
It's about consistency.

It's not about dramatic leaps, but daily alignment.

It's not about who you think you should be, but who you already are beneath the noise.

When you live these eight essentials, change stops being something you chase. It becomes the natural expression of your evolving consciousness.

You no longer "try" to be better.
You simply become more of who you are.

And that, right there, is the quiet revolution —
The ripple that begins within, and moves outward into everything you touch.

REFLECTION EXERCISE

Take a deep breath.
Then choose one of the eight essentials that resonates most for you right now.

Ask yourself:

What does this mean for me today?

What's one small action I can take to embody it?

How will I know I've shifted, even slightly?

Write your answer.
Then act on it — one breath, one choice, one ripple at a time.

Because lasting change doesn't happen by accident.
It happens by alignment.
And every aligned act creates a ripple that reshapes your life — and the lives of others.

CHAPTER 9

The Future Is Yours: The Conscious Choice Point

There comes a moment — often quiet, rarely convenient — when life holds up a mirror and whispers,

"Who are you choosing to be?"

That moment is not out there somewhere in the future.
It's here.
Now.
This breath.

The world doesn't change in conferences or board-rooms or political campaigns.

It changes in moments like this — when one person decides to stop living from fear, and starts living from love.

We are living through one of the most pivotal times in human history.
Technology is accelerating faster than our wisdom.
Connection has never been easier — yet loneliness has never been higher.
The noise of distraction grows louder each day.
And amidst it all, the invitation remains the same:
Wake up.

You Are Not a Victim of the World You See

The old paradigm tells you that you are a product of circumstance — that your environment defines you, your past limits you, and your future depends on luck.

That story is comfortable. It absolves responsibility.
But it's also a lie.

You are not a machine being acted upon.
You are consciousness in motion. You are a creator of the life and world you want to live in. A living, breathing field of awareness and energy capable of creating, healing, and transforming.

When you realise this, everything changes.

You stop waiting for the world to be fair, and start becoming the fairness you seek.
You stop asking when things will improve, and start being the improvement.
You stop searching for light, and start remembering that you are it.

As Viktor Frankl wrote after surviving the unimaginable,

> "Between stimulus and response, there is a space. In that space is our power to choose our response. In our response lies our growth and our freedom."

That space — that conscious pause — is where your ripple begins.

The Choice Point

Every day, you stand at a crossroads between two paths: unconscious reaction or conscious creation.

Reaction is automatic — driven by habit, ego, and fear.
Creation is intentional — guided by awareness, love, and possibility.

Most people live ninety-five percent of their lives in reaction, replaying the same thoughts, emotions, and patterns over and over again, wondering why nothing changes.

But in every moment, you can interrupt the loop.
You can choose awareness over autopilot.
You can choose curiosity over control.
You can choose love over fear.

That single choice — repeated consistently — is the foundation of a revolution.

Not the loud kind.
The quiet kind.
The kind that starts in your breath and ends in your legacy.

From Change to Creation

Change begins when you decide to stop living by default and start living by design.

It begins when you realise that consciousness is creative — that your inner state determines your outer experience.

You can't control what happens in the world, but you can control how you show up in it.
And how you show up changes the field.

The science is clear: your emotional energy influences others, your coherence stabilises groups, your compassion regulates teams.
You are an emitter.
A transmitter.
A creator.

So if you truly want to see a better world — in your organisation, your family, your community — start with your own frequency.

The ripple doesn't ask for perfection.
It asks for presence.

It asks for leaders who are willing to pause, breathe, and bring their humanity to the moment.

Because when you shift your energy, you shift everything.

The Breath of the Revolution

There is one tool that connects it all — one bridge between body, mind, and consciousness.
Your breath.

Each breath is a reminder: you are alive, connected, and capable of renewal in every moment.

When you breathe consciously, you interrupt the stress cycle.
You restore the nervous system.
You reset the field.

A single conscious breath can dissolve a lifetime of conditioning.

That's why I often say:

"Change the world. One breath at a time."

Because it's not the size of your action that changes things — it's the energy behind it.

The AGV Method

Here's a simple daily practice — a way to anchor yourself in the frequency of conscious leadership.

A = Awareness
Close your eyes. Feel your breath. Notice your thoughts without chasing them.
Become aware of your body, your sensations, your aliveness.

G = Gratitude
Shift your focus to your heart. Think of one thing — or one person — you're grateful for.

Let that feeling expand through your chest, your breath, your entire being.

V = Visualisation
Picture your future self — grounded, calm, purposeful. See how they move through the day, how they speak, how they lead.
Then ask: "What would that version of me do next?"

This is not imagination. It's calibration.
You're tuning your energy to the frequency of your highest potential.

Do this daily, even for a few minutes, and watch how your reality begins to reorganise itself around your new vibration.

Legacy Is a Living Thing

Legacy is not what you leave behind when you're gone. It's what you create in the people around you while you're here.

Every conversation is an opportunity to plant seeds of awareness.
Every act of kindness is a ripple that outlives you.

Legacy is not built through ambition, but through alignment.

It's not about how much you achieve, but how much you awaken.

And as you awaken, you become the kind of leader the future needs —
grounded, conscious, connected, compassionate.

Not driven by fear of being forgotten, but by the joy of being alive.

REFLECTION EXERCISE

Take three slow breaths.

Then ask yourself:

What world do I want my ripple to create?

How will I embody that energy today?

What is one action — one breath, one word, one choice — that will move that vision into reality?

Write it down.
Then live it.

Because the future is not waiting for someone else to fix it.
It's waiting for you to remember who you are.

You are the ripple.
You are the revolution.
You are the consciousness that can change the world —

One breath at a time.

Continue the Ripple

If this book has stirred something in you —
a shift in awareness, a new perspective, a deeper question —
then this is your next step.

Because insight is powerful.

But integration is transformational.

Most leadership development focuses on what you do.

The **Limbic Performance System® (LPS)** focuses on what drives you —
your beliefs, emotions, values, and subconscious patterns.

This is where real change happens.

When you develop at this level, everything shifts:

- You respond instead of react
- You lead with calm authority under pressure
- You build trust, openness, and psychological safety
- You handle conflict without escalation
- You align purpose, values, and action
- You create teams that thrive — not just perform

At the heart of LPS is a **12-domain leadership model** — a complete system for developing leadership from the inside out.

And for those ready to go further, the **Legacy Leadership Academy** brings this work to life.

This is not a course.

It is a carefully curated leadership journey — designed for those ready to evolve how they think, feel, and lead.

Because every leader creates a ripple.

The question is:
What kind of ripple are you creating?

Take the Next Step

Scan the QR code or visit:

www.lpszone.com

About the Author

Steve Neale is an international leadership psychologist, executive coach, and founder of the Limbic Performance System for Outstanding Leadership and the Legacy Leadership Academy. His work integrates psychology, neuroscience, and mindfulness to help leaders transform performance from the inside out. A speaker and facilitator to thousands of leaders across Europe and beyond, Steve's mission is simple: to help people lead with greater awareness, compassion and consciousness — changing the world one breath at a time.

Your Ripple Journal

www.ingramcontent.com/pod-product-compliance
Lightning Source LLC
LaVergne TN
LVHW010937110826
845149LV00013B/2631

* 9 7 8 1 0 6 7 6 4 9 4 0 1 *